A Random Caller

Heather Cameron

A Random Caller
Cancer Poetry

Thanks

I thank the wonderful team of healthcare professionals and peers at the Barwon Health Andrew Love Cancer Centre, Wadawurrung Country, Geelong, Victoria, Australia, who supported me and continue to support me through my experience with cancer. It's a wicked disease but it has given me opportunities to live in ways I never would have dreamed of. I am in awe of those who work in the cancer field – I wouldn't be here without their dedicated care, and because of them, I feel blessed every day of my life.

I thank Deakin University for allowing me to complete this collection of poetry as the creative component of my Doctor of Philosophy, awarded in 2021. I sincerely thank Graduate Women Victoria and the Rodriguez family for their invaluable support, via the Judith Rodriguez scholarship, awarded in 2020.

Having acknowledged the reality of my experience with cancer, I remind the reader that these poems are fictional, and in no way are intended to refer to specific individuals, groups, teams or me. I do not intend to imply that I know what each person's experience with cancer is, whether as a sufferer, carer, or health professional. Whatever your experience, I offer my profound respect and good wishes to you.

A Random Caller: Cancer Poetry
ISBN 978 1 76109 525 2
Copyright © text Heather Cameron 2023
Cover image: Yvonne Smith – Kaka Point, The Catlins, NZ

First published 2023 by
GINNINDERRA PRESS
PO Box 3461 Port Adelaide 5015
www.ginninderrapress.com.au

Contents

Hearing the word uttered, then uttered again

   Cancer   11
   Catchphrases at the time of diagnosis   12
   Naming it   14
   A random caller   15
   A letter to my body   16
   We are here   18
   War   19
   Where it starts   20
   The day my husband was diagnosed with cancer   22
   Anatomy of disaster   23
   Waiting   24
   Acknowledging Jane Kenyon   26

Cells shifting, mutating, shifting, mutating, shifting

   My quiet hum   29
   Brain scan   30
   Breast cancer surgeon 1   31
   Breast cancer surgeon 2   32
   Breast cancer surgeon 3   33
   Note to the young doctor   34
   City treatment   35
   In the chemo chair   36
   A death on the way to day chemo   37
   So, what was chemo like?   38
   On the beach   39
   My hair   40
   My charms   41
   Waiting room   42
   Missing   43
   This play of ours   44

Examinations	45
The magpie	46
The inland road	47
Speaking of cancer	48
Hail radiation	49
The Zen of cancer	50
The problem with soup	51
The memory of kindness	52
My witness 2008–09	53

Saw the doctor today, he's sorry but honest

A visit to the cemetery	57
The question of dying	58
Limitations	59
Metastases	60
There goes death	62
Magnolia tree	63
The call	64
Discussing disposal	65
My death apparel	66
Forgiveness	67
These places in heaven	68
How does a mother let go?	69

I listen, hoping to hear, forgetting you're not here

After you died	73
Everything	74
Leave me alone	75
Finding home	76
Now that you're gone	77
Without you here	78
At Xmas	79
You're there	80

Mourning	81
Concert	82
Standing still	83

Now you can get back to normal, you haven't changed a bit

And I quote	87
Inspiration	88
Unrecognisable	89
Known	90
Fear	91
Survivorship	92
The world in a word	94
Our different ways	95
The morning of the annual mammogram	96
After the annual appointment	97
Photo	98
Bramare	99
A brief note to the oncology nurse	100
Mindfulness	101

With my heart I listen to the waves; my *karanga*

I hate that dog	107
Sometimes	108
At Kaka Point	109
At St Helen's Park	110
Something not quite right at St Helen's	111
Stringing words together	114
Walking the perimeter	118
Driving the perimeter	119
All the trees	121
Evening walk during lockdown	122
Caught between	123

Acknowledgements   124

For B.L.
Thank you for the poetry

With eternal thanks to David McCooey,
poet, teacher and friend extraordinaire!

With love to the Squirrels,
Charlotte, Jacqui, Rhett, and Sarah

Hearing the word uttered, then uttered again

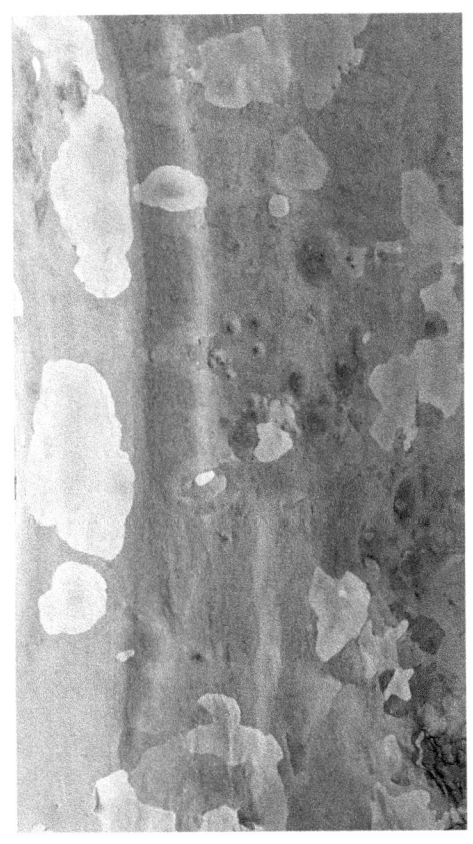

Cancer

The life lived in the body
Was the blood, warm in the veins.
White halos of icy breath,
Frost caught in the sportsground lights.
How you ran and played hard for the team.

It was monsters under the bed,
Shadows on the night windows.
White cold stars in a night sky, shining for us
As we crossed the oval on the way home.
Where we swore our promises of surrender.

It was a growing murmur, the story of
Vows forgotten and loves ending.
White-knuckled fear and shotgun heart,
Sitting in the driveway, clutching the phone.
Hearing the word uttered, then uttered again.

Catchphrases at the time of diagnosis

Chapter 1: What was said to me

It may be nothing sinister, but we'd better get it checked out.
    Let's not panic until we know what it is.
It may be nothing, like the doctor said.
Take everything off above the waist.
Put this gown on, opening to the back.
    This will feel a bit cold, but we need to use the jelly.
(Silence)
We're just looking at the screen.
(Silence)
    We're going to ask the doctor to come and look.
Hello.
I need to do a biopsy immediately.
This will sting a bit. That's right, arm above your head.
Thank you.
Here we go.
(Silence)
I can't say for sure until the test results are back but it's looking nasty.
Very nasty.
You're here alone, aren't you?
Are you all right to drive home?
We need to wait for the test results.
We don't know for sure yet.
There's no point in worrying about something that hasn't happened yet.
Hello.
The biopsy's confirmed that it's breast cancer.

Chapter 2: What I said in response

(Silenced)
(Silent)
(Silence)

Naming it

My doctor's straight with me.
He knows how to say more than the words
I need to hear. Like the time he rang me to say, *it's breast cancer.*

He didn't say, *I'm sorry, you have breast cancer,* like it was some gift
He was reluctantly delivering to my door. Something I had to own.

He began the surgical cut when he called the damn thing 'it'.
Gave it lower case letters to put it where it belonged.

He named it and helped me keep it small. Despite its size.
He knew not to say, *I'm sorry.* Even though he was.

A random caller

You open the door and there it is,
And even if you were half expecting it,

It still surprises you to find cancer at *your* door.
Rudely pushing its way inside,

It grabs you by the throat,
Pins you up against the wall.

Steals that thought you didn't know you had;
The one that said, you're too good for this kind of bad.

Picks you up and tumbles you over
In a fiery, erratic ballet.

Dances you into the world of prognosis,
With its haunting prophetic metre.

Leaves you wishing you could have
Slammed the door on this horrifying stranger.

Just some random, I shout,
When my son calls, *who was that at the door?*

A letter to my body

Dear Body, how could you?
How could you turn on me like this?
So silently and stealthily,
You have generated this cancerous growth.
Deep inside your cavernous darkness,
You have been harbouring
A cellular rebellion of such magnitude,
It has shaken us to the core.

Dear Vessel of Infinite Mystery,
Is this some form of random revenge?
I know I haven't cared for you as I should,
The myriad of substances and craziness,
The coldness of strangers' beds,
The colder continent of home.
But all these years I've been coming back
From the brink, and now you do this?

Dear Body, how do we go on?
How do I trust you to carry me now?
I loathe your reflection in the mirror,
You have become misshapen and lumpish.
I drag your diseased mass to the clinic,
Present you as another stricken specimen
To the doctors; magicians who look kindly,
Who palpate and probe, searching for your sins.

And now you're reproaching me and rightly so,
It is me who drags you into the hell of
Chemo, the public unmasking of all that you are.
I insist you weather the pouring of these toxic
Medicines, knowing how much it destroys.
Wiping your slate clean, banishing the
Mutation, ignoring your cries of pain,
Your stunned abandonment and shame.

Oh, my Body, we have lost each other in this chaos.
I've raged against the proliferation of deadly cells,
You have earnestly, frantically produced,
And you have recoiled at the cutting, poisoning,
Burning lifelines I've thrown to you.
How do we go on from here, you and me?
Is the long-awaited reunion to be denied?
Is now to be the time I lose you to the grave?

We are here

We are here:

Mum, I can't find my school jumper.
        You put tomato on my sandwiches!

I need money for the excursion today.
        Where's my maths homework?

I left my sports gear in my locker.
        Do we have to go to after school care today?

And then we are not:

But you don't even look sick.
        I hate hospitals. I don't want you to go.

I don't understand why you got it.
        It's not fair. I don't think it's fair.

I'm going to jump on the trampoline.
        Mum, who will look after us if you die?

War

No poet would deign to mimic the media,
As they expatiate the battles fought and lost.
Heroism based on some notion of choice.

So it is with disdain, she resists the metaphors,
Until the middle of the night
When she writes, Cancer is a war!

A battleground of sterilised, white-walled trenches,
Stoic troops waiting amongst the paraphernalia
Of war machinery, and chemical weaponry.

The relatives weeping in the churches,
Pray and wait for news. Ponder how this war
Came to breach their once secure borders.

And as the battle unfolds, as the war is waged,
She wanders naked and alone, a refugee,
Unable to find her way home.

Come morning, she packs up the night's scribbles,
Sprays her wig with conditioner, restores her
Disguise. Camouflages the collateral damage.

Where it starts

The New Holland honeyeaters build a nest
In a fir tree, under the eye of
The calico cat. Sleek and replete,
She curls into sleep.

The sun spears the distant edges,
Smoky haze, and the birds sing.
It's a nest-building song,
And the cat's tail twitches in time.

The phone rings.
Words crackling with a wilding wind.
He's ringing from the beach,
He's seen the doc; the results are in.

I'm afraid it's not looking good.
There is a shadow in the lung.
A shadow in the lung.
A shadow. In the lung.

Sun dips below the ridge,
Birds fall silent among the
Silent, unmoving fir trees.
Evening cold moves swiftly.

There is the crunching sound of
Scree, where I walk. The cat
Retires inside, curls up,
Dreams of hunting.

The world recedes into shadow.
Shadows commandeer the path.
Lace the trees into forest,
Losing each other to the dark.

The day my husband was diagnosed with cancer

Early on the morning of the day he got the diagnosis,
He went around the house pulling down the blinds,
Providing a running monologue about the Australian heat.
He was like a captain battening down the hatches, while I
Prepared a thermos, like any crew member would do.

Mid-morning on the day he got the diagnosis,
He paced between the corridor and the waiting room,
Bemoaning the long waiting times one must endure
In the Australian public health system. An angry buzzing fly,
Batting himself against the glass, while I sat very still,
Parched throat; the forgotten, abandoned flask in the car.

Early in the afternoon of the day he got the diagnosis,
He sat staring at the doctor, one hand balled into a fist
And the other clasped in mine, repeating the question,
How long have I got? His lazy-vowel drawl at odds with it all.
A beggar, losing hope on the street, light in his eyes dying,
And all I could think was, where did I leave that blasted tea?

Anatomy of disaster

After her son's death, she turned to Moore's advice;
(Tend body, tend home, tend mind, tend connections, tend spirit).
And now she has learnt to not drop at the sight of visitors on the path,
When those who care for her, come to offer comfort and cheer.

She has found the peace the moon lays as a trail on the black sea,
And the sand shifting with the tidal flooding at the river mouth.
The rain drenching the ground turns the garden wild, the bush
Sends down mists filled with scents that pinch at her nostrils.

And in the evening light, just as the sunset throws pink across the sky,
She coughs the blood into her handkerchief, feels the pain in her chest;
Familiar yet alien. Like the sea continuing the same old story,
But each day bringing news of the uncontrollable world.

Waiting

I

The old man in the
Cancer clinic waiting room
Reads the newspaper
As though he is sitting
At his kitchen table,
With a cup of tea
In front of him.

He turns the page
And shakes the paper,
Irritating the old woman
Sitting near him.
Not that he would know,
As he lies buried from
The waist up, behind

The large sheets of
Carbon-covered pages,
Engrossed in the horrors
And the workings of
The world as told to
Him by the men and
Women of the AWP.

His hand appears from
Behind the paper,
Reaches for his cup of tea,
Which isn't there.
He clicks his false teeth
In disgust, shakes the paper,
Mutters about having to wait.

II

Yesterday, at the baby shower, a woman said,
How bitter-sweet it must be that new life
Was on the way, while she was fighting for her own.

Today, she smiles at the elderly lady sitting
In the waiting room, sees the questioning stare
At her swollen belly. Looks away, too tired to say.

A cup of tea would help, she thinks. Rubs her belly,
Winces, then yawns, as the baby kicks.
I'm sick of waiting too, little one.

Cancer is just a disease she tells her little family.
What's more important in life, is love, the willingness
To go on. Weeps, when they are sleeping.

Acknowledging Jane Kenyon

In Finland they talk of cancer,
How it bites *(nakertaa)* and rots *(mädättää)*.
Metaphorically speaking, we all do.
The malignant beast, unseen, stealthily grows.

Still searching for the right word,
I skirt the edge of the bay.

Heavy grey sky, the white chests of
The cormorants glowing luminous.
Resting like ghosts on the pylons
Running out from the shore,
They shimmer above the black water.

Cells shifting, mutating, shifting, mutating, shifting

My quiet hum

Piped music in
The waiting room,
A Beatles tune.

Vibrating hum,
Snatches of song,
Deep in my body.

Tickets to the MCG,
Paul McCartney,
So easy to be

Alive! Autumn night,
Stage lights,
And the city sky.

Don't be afraid.
It's just deep down,
Under the song,

Cells shifting,
Mutating, shifting,
Mutating, shifting.

Diminishing me.
Morphing my life.
My quiet hum.

Brain scan

The radiographer sits silently in her booth.
Blue-green screens reflect across her face.
Leaves me to the quiet machinations of the CT beam,
As it crosses back and forth, rhythmically recording
The mysteries of my meagre, human brain.

Can she see the kaleidoscope's shattered glass?
The poem; a silver trail of a cerebral jet stream,
Lit now and then by an occasional burst of light?
Are the flowering lavender the purple waves captured,
Riding the blue between sea and sky?
And the jacaranda trees; do they stand calmly?

Can she see the two oaks that have grown into each other?
Old branches entwined in a dignified embrace.
Has she caught sight of the kea, black against
Snow-white alps, riding the alpine updrafts?
And surely, the black cat pads by,
Looks into the lens, and resumes his night hunting?

Breast cancer surgeon 1

The surgeon tells me he picked apricots in Central Otago.
He was a young medical student on a summer break.
Near retirement now, his scalpel an extension of his hand.

I remember we bought a case of apricots, newly picked.
The reeking kitchen as my mother made the preserves,
Thick with sugary syrup. Hot apricot sponge, and custard.

Standing in the cold, dark shed, counting bottles and jars
Lined up on the shelves. The crock of preserved eggs below.
Snow cleared from the open doorway. Beyond, the kitchen lights.

Breast cancer surgeon 2

The reverence with which
You lay your scalpel
Upon my skin
Is reminiscent of a lover
From long ago.

You cut delicately, assuredly
Your blade tracing
A predetermined line
And enter my body
Just as he did.

I signed consent forms
For your loving invasion.
What choice had I?

He took my clasp upon
His hips as permission.
What choice had he?

My body has been laid
Open by the knives of
Lovers and surgeons alike.
Scars chosen/unchosen,
Fade red into ochre lines.

Breast cancer surgeon 3

Oh, masterful Surgeon,
Strolling the corridors of pain.
Passing the inanely smiling woman,
Gifting the solemnity of a 'hi'.

Come, let's you and I not be coy,
Let's you and I be sensual in our dance.
We are, after all, old lovers of a sort,
Or has this body escaped your memory?

Oh, great Master of the healing knives,
You with the long lean fingers,
Latex gloves smooth and slippery,
You have been inside my body.

You have been inside my body.
With finesse and a delicate cut,
You have carefully taken a part of me,
You have left me on the table in pieces.

Note to the young doctor

Doctor, oh doctor, doing your rounds,
Your voice carries when you walk the ward.
We lopped off the breast you say to the students,
Who nod and scribble and scurry around.

There you are; an arborist in some parallel universe,
Carelessly lopping the branches from trees.

Dis-en-gage, dis-en-gage, dis-en-gage,
I chant to myself in three four time.

Lit-tle-pup.
Lit-tle-pup.
Lit-tle-pup.

How are you today, you ask, pseudo adult-you,
I grunt a reply, yes, GRUNT a reply,
You stiffen, make notes, and with a jerk
Of your head, gesture the students away.

Oh, little pup,
don't you know?
don't you know?

I was a gorgeous woman with magnificent breasts!
I had lovers galore who treasured me all,
We sipped wine, drank of life, and more.

And what does that count for now, for now?
What does that count for now?

City treatment

I'm told I'll get used to
The incessant noise of the traffic
That thunders down the street
Where this city hospital lies.

*You won't even hear the trams
Any more,* I'm told airily.

Late at night, I lie awake,
Screaming sirens, blue and alive,
Streaming from the emergency bay,
On the way to rescue someone.

I miss the quiet surge of the sea,
That gentle-wave whisper.

Discontent nests in my body,
Words stick in an oesophageal jam.
I await the early morning ward round,
Night-dreaming about going home.

In the chemo chair

The space between you and the world
Is bridged daily by the calico cat,
Who purrs you into a semblance
Of breath, which the yoga teacher
Herself would aspire to.

But there you are, brimming over
With thoughts, and piling
Words into the spaces that you had
Planned to keep wide open.

And all the while Chopin makes music
Sound like rain on the woolshed roof,
Under which you lay huddled in
The greasy bale, where you allowed yourself to be.
Where you opened your arms to the sky.

A death on the way to day chemo

The slenderness of the young woman
Belies the courage she possesses,
As she runs into the middle of the intersection,
Scoops up the stunned little ginger body.
Cradles it against her designer shirt.

She blinks long, mascaraed eyelashes,
And passes me the burden of a race to the vet.
Nestled in the black blanket, warm little body,
Broken, its blue eyes staring,
Its mouth open in a final mew.

He's still warm, the vet says,
Describes catastrophic injuries,
Inevitable death.
Adds in her no-nonsense, offhand way,
You did all you could do.

*

The nurse who checks the chemo bag
Wears no makeup; chats to us all.
Fiercely clean, efficient and kind,
A lifeboat of blue-gowned proportions,
She sails amongst us maroons in this toxic sea.

I wonder if she would have the courage to
Scoop me up off the floor, to lay me against her cotton chest.
If she would turn calmly to the shocked young doctor,
And say gently, over my still warm body,
We did all we could do.

So, what was chemo like?

Poisons sweep my landscape,
Attack in true heroic style.
Become a flaming bush of thorns,
My own thicket of hell.

If I allow myself to see the thorns,
Their pink nails will grow beyond my control,
And this strange stabbing world I inhabit
Will become all that I know and am known by.

I pace. I pace.
Walking might help the toxins move through your body.

I sit.
You will need to rest and let the chemo do its work.

I lie in the bath.
Floating.

Three days and it passes.
Three weeks and the mantra steadies me as I go.
I welcome this healing medicine into my body.
And the toxic flood begins again.

I sight the thicket world ahead.
I know this place,
This lifesaving hell you send me to,
With a smile, and a cheery word.

Please know me beyond these borders.
Please remember who I am.
A fervent whisper, as much to myself as to you,
As I enter my thorny-thicket hell.

On the beach

The world is reduced in the chemo day ward; a busy, enclosed space, far removed from the outside world. And I have been reduced as well – I have become this small, hushed, passive woman, sitting still in the chemo chair, being a good patient, taking my medicine.

In the distance the long arm of a crane rises
Out of the sand dunes, above the new houses,
And you ponder the places where tumours grow.

On the beach, billowing white clouds with their
Swollen underbellies, bruised and black.
You shout your noise to the waves roaring in,

And they roar back, recoil, rush at you again.
Out here, your voice is a primal earth-beat,
Echoing out over the sea-foamed turmoil,

Out to the ragged horizon, and beyond.
All the Universe is filled, gloriously
Filled, with the rowdiness that is you.

My hair

Margaret shaves my head
With slow delicate sweeps
Of the silver shaver.
Her face in our shared reflection
Has fine soft lines
Where her smile sits.

You won't know yourself
With your new wig,
Margaret says gently,
And she's right.

My charms

I take seven lucky charms to the chemo ward,
In a green satin pouch with gold printed dragons.

Two have angels stamped on their silver sides,
With *hope* and *harmony* crooked on their backs.

These ones were sent by my mother, sent flying
Across water, across greater distances between us.

Two have angels sitting, resting doves in their hands,
and www.pocketangels.com engraved on their backsides.

You picked two up in a dairy along with your smokes and
A Coke, tossed them to me as you drove to the clinic.

Your mother arrived with the gold one, the hovering angel,
Offered chicken soup (no bones of course), and tears.

I jiggle the charms in the little green pouch, waiting for
The nurse to insert the needle. For the magic to begin.

Waiting room

You sat beside me in the waiting room
And one of us started the conversation.
I was early-stage and on to my second chemo.
You had returned after two years, resigned to
Stepping back on the treatment cycle.

I shrank away ever so slightly from you.
I didn't want to hear words like advanced,
Secondaries and relapse. Superstition dried
Up my chat, as though hearing your bad news
Would diminish the optimism I was being
Coached to wear; would jeopardise my chances.

I saw you a few weeks later, vomiting into
A sick bag while you waited at the front door
For a taxi. Your husband was sitting at the other end
Of the seat, looking out over the rooftops to nowhere.

Missing

The woman sitting beside me in the chemo ward,
Leans over and tells me that cancer is the best thing
That has happened to her. *I found myself*,
She says, with a meaningful nod.

Sitting on that ill-gotten throne, swallowing metals,
I allow the evangelist to open the wound.
In surrender, I whisper to her closed face,
I lost myself.

Pinpricks of chemo on fire,
And I ponder when it was,
That I became someone,
I now list as missing?

Was it that moment in the bathroom,
Taking a morning shower, fingers returning
Again, and again, in disbelief
To that pea-sized aberration?

Or was it later, when, my name erased,
I became the breast cancer patient?
When each kind, and competent staff member,
Handled my breast, with impersonal intimacy?

This play of ours

Take away the white coat and the stethoscope.
Are you as naked as I am?

This play we rehearse has such quaint roles.
You cut a striking figure as the leading man.

I set the scene in the waiting room, but
My supporting role is barely worth a glance.

You walk through your sterile lines
With your practised look of empathy.

Not knowing as the amateur would know,
Improvisation would open me as a flower.

No matter; no stage direction will explain.
I am far away. Running through canola fields.

Examinations

I

I lie on a table in a darkened room,
The sonographer locks the door, saying
She knows how intrusive this will be.
Thrusts the cold metal instrument deep inside me,
Impassively searches the black and white images.

II

I lie on a bed, bright light above,
The doctor methodically explores each breast,
Searching in quadrants, now the abdomen,
The line of my collar bone. Lips pursed, eyes intent.
Good she murmurs, stepping back.

III

At the pool, I swim, arm over arm, counting
My breaths, my strokes like a heartbeat,
My arms sweeping an arc in the heated air,
In the water, I see brown, feathery body-wings.
On examination, I marvel at their perfection.

The magpie

Outside the Cancer Centre
A magpie stood before me.
We shared an unblinking stare.

She threw back her head,
Sang a single line of purity.

I cradled it,
Sitting in the chemo chair,
A line embedded in my vein.

The inland road

And the inland road I take to the clinic
Is a dark and windy, potholed shame,
But I like it all the same.

Its bush-clad verges shout *Out,*
Like the mountains the snowplough left
When it came to clear a path for us to leave
The farm. The hurrah of being able to get out!

Despite knowing you could never leave.

Don't look back, I chide,
As I miss the turn-off to
The inland road.

This new, straight dart of a freeway is fine,
With its wide expanse, black-fast bitumen, and
White snake-lines. It goes on and on.

Ah well, this speed will get me there early,
Always good to sit and wait. To breathe.

And the dried-up yellows of the fields flash by,
No memories of escape in their irradiated planes.

Speaking of cancer

I speak of loss, though
At the corners of the nightmare,
There may be words of light,
Even laughter.

You talk of science,
As I scan your face
For the subtle cues that might
Promise cure.

Hail radiation

In the radiation cave,
I say five Hail Marys,
As the burning beam
Does its cleansing sweep
Of the tattooed segments.

I'd planned to use the Navajo chant,
But here I am at the first
Sign of the radiant beam,
Calling out to Mother Mary,
To save this sinner at
The hour of this death.

We are patient, Mary and I,
We get used to waiting.
We get to understand,
That saving and being saved

Is a slow
And tedious business.

The Zen of cancer

Practicing her Zen meditation,
She trips into the core; simply laughter.

Hears it echo in her body, bouncing against
The dark; filling the empty halls.

Nothing is. Pain and aching body,
All nothing. The freedom to be

In the comical darkness; being
Nothing, and nothing, she becomes.

Driving to the radiotherapy centre,
Seatbelt sets her burnt chest on fire.

Fatigue hits as she sits at the traffic lights.
The world is a red light.

She imagines the driver behind her, telling the paramedic,
This woman just fell asleep at the wheel; caused havoc.

The world turns green; she accelerates away.
Takes a blinding headache through the intersection.

Arriving, she carefully arranges nothing
In a neat pile outside the doors.

De-activating her Romulan-like cloaking device,
She uncovers. Is revealed.

The problem with soup

Spicy carrot and parsnip soup sits in a bowl.
I time the microwave oven to 2.00
But just when it has 15 seconds to go,
I hit the Stop/Cancel button twice, in quick succession.

Why did you stop it early?
Your voice arrives behind me in that tone
You've found to mark my descent into helplessness.

It won't be hot enough now, you say,
As you manoeuvre around me,
Taking command of the whole soup situation.

I wish you would let me help you, you say.
It's not a failure to accept help, you know.
You've spent your life helping others,
Now it's our turn to help you.

The microwave pings in agreement.

Actually, I don't feel like soup, I say,
Dry retching as I walk away.

The memory of kindness

Miss Hannah of the long black hair,
Minidress and the knee-high white boots.

Sitting on the mat at her feet,
Alive with tales of Julian, Dick, George and Anne,
And Timmy the dog, of course.

The temptation to lay your cheek against
The white vinyl-clad calves.

The mystery of a black nylon line
Running between skirt and boot top.

The tears one morning, the rings
On her fingers chafing your frozen hands,
As she rubbed the blood back to life.

You didn't know you would say,
This is the first memory of kindness.

Just as you didn't know how to tell
The nurse that sat beside your chemo chair.

Reminded you of a Cornish coastline,
And children, strong and brave,
Defeating danger.

My witness 2008–09

Old man sitting
In his old ute
At the beach.
Jerks his chin up in that greeting
Australian men do. Foreign,
But I take it anyway.

> Watches me walk the sand-stretch of Fishos,
> The stitches prickle; pinpoints of fire,
> Wetness in my armpit, seeping away.
>
> Sits there to see me falter halfway,
> The tide line frilled with seaweed, entangling
> Wisps of hair blowing from my head.
>
> Looks away as I buckle, bone-deep weights,
> The bandanna flicking about my bald head,
> Breath whipped away in the biting sea breeze.
>
> Watches me make the long trek to a tidal edge,
> Fuzzy growth on my head rippling,
> Like wheat-waves in an unseasonal wind.

>> Old man sitting
>> In his old ute
>> At the beach.
>> Raises his hand in a salute,
>> Grins; stares out over the reef
>> To the crumbling cliffs at Point Danger.

Saw the doctor today, he's sorry but honest

A visit to the cemetery

I came to say
We'll be having that reunion soon.
Saw the doctor today,
He's sorry but honest.

Now it's all about
Putting one's affairs in order,
As though the disorder
Was ever ours to choose.

I've got time to regret,
To say goodbye.
Unlike you in your mad rush.
Gone.

Puzzling to think you,
Always travelling at ludicrous speeds,
Might be content to rest
In this stillness now.

To lie beside you
In this peaceful place.
Clouds in the uneven blue,
And sunlight.

How quiet it is, between
The reaching shadows.
Until a magpie calls,
Somewhere from among the fir trees.

The question of dying

I cannot find the words
To ask the oncologist,
So, I leave the question
Unspoken.

I ask the arborist though,
Is the tree dying?
He looks up, mutters
Doubtfully.

In these grey winter days
The tree retreats
Into skeletal black limbs,
Sleeping.

*

Come spring, the oncologist
Says, *I have good news.*
My cancer markers
Have dropped.

Buds appear overnight,
Within a week, the lush
Canopy fills the sky,
Aue, te rakau!

Kia ora, I whisper
To the green leaves,
The pockfaced bark,
Warm in the sun.

Limitations

I sit opposite you, comment on how
Red the sunrise was this morning,
Ask if you saw it on your way to work.

You smile, bemused and say no,
You started early, in the dark,
Important clinical meetings before outpatients.

And you add that you're not even sure
Where east is in this town. You shrug,
Fiddle with the stethoscope around your neck.

And I can't help but blurt out that
Taking time to see the sunrise is important.
That your sense of direction might improve

If you lifted your head and looked to the sky.
You smile. One of those smiles
Young men often bestow on old women.

You tell me there are more important things
To discuss. Side effects and symptoms,
Degenerative impacts to my diet and movement.

The timely necessity to debate
Choosing the quality of life over quantity.
My point exactly, I reply.

Metastases

Scene: doctor's consulting room.

Doctor (pointing at infographic):
Bone metastases occur when cancer cells break away from the original tumour and spread to the bones, where they multiply.

Patient (appearing to listen calmly):
So basically, you're saying the cancer has spread to my bones now?

Doctor (nodding his head, empathic eye contact):
Yes, the cancer has spread to your bones. It's called metastases.

Patient (nodding):
Right.

*

To roll the word,
Metastases
Around in my mouth,
To spit it out.

To make room for
The little white pills,
Which crumble between
My shaking fingers.

*

Scene: kitchen table.

Man (pointing to doctor's infographic):
He said the cancer has spread to my bones. It's called metastases.

Woman (frowning, shocked expression):
I don't understand, he said the chemo had shrunk the tumour. How can it have spread to your bones? What does it mean?

Man (quietly, looking out kitchen window):
It means I'm fucked.

There goes death

The experts on death imply
I'll get there before they do,
So confident in their prognostic skill,
As if they never step off street corners,
And cars never run red lights, accelerating.

The way it's written about, spoken about, whispered about,
Dreamt. One would think it's a destination to get to.

More a wounded bull, and me wearing red as I do.
Blood and bone, and a sprinkling of wisdom is what I have today.

The regurgitated worm food
Will be black on the soil tomorrow,
Or the ashes will blow where you throw;
Out to sea if you please.

And in the end, it won't be mine or theirs.
I like to think it will be free.

Nothing to do, nothing to be.
Simply hanging in the cool coastal sky.

Magnolia tree

You used to laugh when you saw me
Crossing the days off the calendar.
Yet, when I was given the prognosis,
It was you who asked, *how long have we got?*

I've stopped drawing neat lines through the days.
Instead, I walk in the garden at dawn.
I sit on the wooden bench under the magnolia,
Its delicate, lilac-coloured blooms overhead.

Winter is passing, spring is stealing its way
Into the orchard on warm, sea-scented winds.
The flowers are falling from the magnolia tree,
Staining the ground with their purpled passing.

The call

I'm dying.

We're all dying, you retort, as though
You've taken a bullet meant for me.

But this bullet is mine. There will be no
Walking hand in hand into this black tunnel.

It's not yours to explore, and
I have no desire to travel in tandem.

I have no thirst for the adventure.
The fatigue takes me at the oddest times,

And I see things in the tunnel ahead.
The other world calls me to come away.

Discussing disposal

But why would you want to be buried, he asks,
When it means decomposing into brown slime
And feeding the worms, and basically, well yuk!

But I wouldn't be there to know it, I reply,
I'd be released from my shell and I like to think
The spirit-me will be walking on some heavenly beach.

You think it's going to be OK for me to visit your grave
And have to stand there and imagine you lying
Beneath my feet, all bones and rotting flesh, he protests.

Can you not think of my body as being separate to me?
Can you not imagine me walking on that beach, rather than
Being the body that's dead and buried in the grave, I ask.

No, I don't want to think of your body being dead,
How can I do that when your body is how I know you now?
Am I supposed to just let you go, when it's all I know?

My death apparel

How to tell the Grim Reaper
That his robes lend an elegance
Not altogether fitting to his role?

That one might envy the woven fabric,
And ache for its loosely folding softness
On a ravaged body, such as mine.

I would gladly give to him
This stinking, sore-infected skin that
Peels away from me; purulent weeping.

It would surely conjure more realism, more
Recognition, were he to wear this outer me,
When late at night, he walks this hospital floor.

Forgiveness

The whispered confession before you died,
Was the first time you had spoken of your father's sin.
Your fear of dying had nothing to do with the living,
It was all about the terror of meeting him again.

The priest held your hand, spoke of a god who offers
Safety and salvation to all; you sighed peacefully,
And slipped away, left us to your deathly silence,
To the detritus that goes with the end.

Tidying away your life, I wondered if you believed
That the god who could not keep you safe on earth,
Would so easily do so in heaven? Or if your sigh was for
The priest, who foolishly spoke of forgiveness.

These places in heaven

You didn't expect to catch anything,
That day we went fishing off the Queenscliff pier.

Seemed it had always been about running away,
About sitting for hours, with your father.

You talked about memorising the horizon,
For when you stumbled across it in heaven.

How you would say, oh yes, I know this place.
This is our place, me and my dad's.

You'd make a celestial joke to an accompanying angel,
About how you never caught anything.

Before the alcoholism.
Before the cancer.

Did I think there would be these places in heaven?
Places where you'd call out into the sky, *I'm home.*

We probably should have been talking about
How to say goodbye to your father.

But you kept returning to how you would find
These places in heaven; these places that knew you.

I see now, how seduced we were by the light on the water.
How we ignored the electrical storm building black across Sorrento.

How does a mother let go?

I was told,
> *She doesn't believe her son is dying.*

I was told,
> *Do something about it, before it is too late.*

I was told,
> *If she doesn't start behaving, we will take him from her.*

Place him in the care of the state,
Deny her custody.

Place him in protective care,
So that he can die peacefully without her.

Place him in a safe space,
Beyond her incessant demands he fight this cancer.

We stood in the hospital corridor and I asked you,
> *What do you know?*

We stood in the hospital corridor and you told me,
> *I know my son is dying.*

We stood in the hospital corridor and you cried,
> *How does a mother let go?*

The last thing your son said to them was,
> *I want to die at home.*

The last thing your son said to me was,
> *Look after Mum for me.*

The last thing your son heard, as he died, was you;
> *It's okay to let go now, my love.*

I listen, hoping to hear,
forgetting you're not here

After you died

Some person who knows trees
Built this uneven path to wind
Its way through the stand of firs.
Just when my thoughts were on
That bleak straight of assuming
This is what life does to you.

The visiting minister spoke of
A bend in the road as an
Invitation to let go,
To trust the road map
To some god on intimate terms
With absence.

You said you knew
What you were doing,
Where you were going.
I wanted to shout,
Why do *you* always get to choose?
Wasted protest, given
The white flag in your hands.

The patient navigator asked
If I knew how I might forgive you,
No mention of god, thank god.
These firs whisper something in
Their wind-shifting language.
I listen, hoping to hear.
Forgetting, you're not here.

Everything

If I could take that last breath,
Cup it gently in my hands,
Breathe lightly on to it,
To fan some flame of life,
Would I do so?

I hesitate to wish you alive,
When living was unendurable.
Long before the end, you were pain;
In much the same way now,
I am inconsolable loss.

The battle you did with ending life,
Seemingly oblivious to what I endured.
Or was death just a narcissistic denouement?
There on the deathbed, did you look past me,
And see that you were everything?

Leave me alone

Can this be my plea to the gods who took you so young?
Because I don't want to rage on into the night
As I have done on the nights before
This black-as-death, moonless one.

I don't want to console myself with some
Godforsaken belief that there was meaning in any of
The suppurating wounds that held
Your brokenness together.

I don't want to praise all that you were,
And the rest that I imagined you to be.
I don't want to liken your demise to a setting sun,
Or some other ridiculous ending, to make meaning

Of a rendered wound that is utterly, brutally senseless.

There is nothing in this cold night sky
But a splattering of white smeary stars,
Not one of them bright enough to pin you to.
You are nowhere in the blackness. You are beyond finding.

And yet, you are in me and over me,
Under me and through me; my aching knows your touch.
Damn you. Leave me alone. Don't go.
Leave me alone. Don't go.

Finding home

On a beach, smooth and hardened
By a relentless grey sea,
I shouted, *this could be home!*

You shook your head, but I knew
It was you who etched *heaven* in the sand,
Watched as the tide stole the letters away.

And the billy-swinging bus driver
Still stands on the banks above,
Sings 'Waltzing Matilda' as he
Churns the tea until it's as black
As the night skies we left behind.

As black as the hole
I watched you disappear into.

Now that you're gone

They called at midnight
To say you'd died.
So typical of you
To wake me with that.

The cliffs at Urquhart's Bluff
Still rise scaly red, but I haven't come
Across a moon trail like the one
That took us down into Anglesea.

Now that you're gone, there's no one
To know the parts of me I brought with us.
You and the big black cat; the big adventure.
Was he there when you rounded the corner?

I wish you could've held it together.
It was always me who was accused of leaving!
You didn't play fair. Checkmate; your whisper,
Always above the white, wind-ripped waves.

Without you here

I see you pass, just in that moment
When the crowd ahead parts; I see you!
Fleeting. I return to your photo by the bed,
And dream of you and the big black cat.

And that green land I told you would be home.
Not understanding that you both had other plans,
Leaving me as you did, with very little to guard
Against the strange new world in my heart.

Stealthy and silent, cat-green eyes watch me
In my dream, and even in my waking moments.
I move my hand across the lymphatic flesh.
Yes, the fear is rock and pillar in this landscape,

But I persist, fight daily to hold on to the dream.
I talk to the outside world about you being gone,
Pretending that without you here, I am alone.
Passing this way, you leave me, again. Bereft.

At Xmas

Sue rang, *what are you doing for Xmas?*
Intent on saving me from despair,
Refusing to accept my lack of care.
Forced me out to the garage,
And into this dusty debris,
Of packed-away Xmas boxes.

The pink lady ornaments.
God, I'd forgotten!
You packed these away that last Xmas.
Said, *when I'm gone,*
I want you to hang these in memory of me –
Not the cancer.

Here's the packet of little wooden hearts
That Sue sent, the month before you left.
'Heartbroken' she'd written on the card.

Hearts can mend,
I remember you saying.

You're there

In 'Spiegel im Spiegel', the cello singing a man's grief.
In the one-eye-open sleeping cat, curled under
The side of the house where dandelions rule.
In the thrum of rain on the corrugated-iron roof.

In the long drive to the coast because beach walking helps.
In the green-blue crème de menthe of the curving wave,
Just as it breaks and is broken by the black seal, surfing.
And the stillness of the Norfolk pines, roots reaching deep.

In the welcome home from the rainbow lorikeets screeching
Joy into song lines in the creaking, heat-blistering eucalypts.
In the stretching cat, delicately turning her back to amplify
Her dismissal; repayment for the lack of tuna, and a reminder.

Mourning

Dust gathers in the corners of
This room where I lay my head upon
The lavender scented pillow.
(A remedy prescribed by the doctor).

Oh tired and mournful night,
I greet you in this purple-haze,
A mutual, wide-eyed wakefulness,
Tracing the arc of moonlight.

Black bats, silently catching the
Edges, shadows passing by.
If only I had sonar to guide my way.
(Would I find you somewhere out there?)

Concert

Dame Kiri Te Kanawa, 1990

Hagley Park in Christchurch,
Cold night, stars lost above us.

It was bigger than anything,
More than ever. I swayed

At the piercing arc of chest pain,
At the visceral purity.

O mio babbino caro,
Oh my heart, my heart.

Leaving as a flowing river towards the
Narrow gate, a sea of strangers,

Someone began, *Pack up your troubles,*
And you shouted, *smile, smile, smile!*

O mio babbino caro,
Wrapped in the final notes now,

Our sons will smile at the end,
But there is no one who will remember

Like you would have. If those demons
Hadn't beckoned. Hadn't carried you away.

Standing still

I

The sea sounds in
The eucalypts;
Wind waves in leaves.

A silvery cormorant,
Transparent in the glare;
The sun-striped bay.

The dachshund pursuing a
Lone, outraged seagull;
Perfect arc of flight.

And somewhere to the south,
You walk. Salt on your lips.
Lighthouse growing ahead.

Standing still; it stands,
Storm winds and danger,
And still it stands, white.

II

Your feet, your rocky, earth-bound feet,
Your solid, rooted feet,
Sand leached away from purple-white skin,
Tide pulling, tide running.

If you stand before this sea,
For the rest of your life,
I will search for the black bones of petrified
Love; washed clear in the moving swell.

III

Ah grief, my old friend, come
Wrap yourself around me!
Be the outer blackness for the
World to see; shadow of myself.

I will light the inner flame,
Name the white sand where bones lie;
Mourning. Watch for the light ahead,
Standing still; the lighthouse grows.

Now you can get back to normal, you haven't changed a bit

And I quote

You must get sick of people asking how you are.
The big C. God, how awful. Sooner you, than me.

I didn't know you smoked. How much do you drink?
But you're so fit and healthy, are you sure they're right?

My cousin read about sharks and their cartilages,
I'll get you the internet address. More natural than chemo.

You know you got cancer because you care too much.
You stress too much. You ate too much. You didn't eat enough

Organic garlic scones. My naturopath had cancer and
She ate raw and drank juice. You should give her a call.

Have you got a family history? They say it's genetic.
Makes you wonder what you did in a previous life.

You look terrible. You don't look sick. You look so grey.
You're so brave, I couldn't do what you're doing.

My sister worked right through all her treatment.
You've taken leave? Really? You must be bored.

My mother had breast cancer; she died.
Our cat had cancer. Our neighbour's niece had cancer too.

Oh, I didn't recognise you. You've changed so much.
Now you can get back to normal. You haven't changed a bit.

Inspiration

The celebrity brought in to inspire us
Stands at the podium,

Makes a joke about her body
After breast cancer.

I laugh with the rest of them,
Look down at my clenched fists

Resting on my clenched knees.
I am inspired but I am not ready

To laugh about my body
After breast cancer.

Unrecognisable

She spends hours choosing what to wear.
Buys a new outfit because nothing fits anymore.

She's glad there's a halo of fuzzy hair,
Instead of the bald, shiny skull.

Plasters the make-up on carefully, to cover
The shattered skin, the stubby eyebrows.

She stands in front of the mirror. Thinks,
I look better than I did last month.

Ignores the whisper in her head that adds,
I don't even recognise you any more.

*

She walks in the door, wanting to walk out.
Holds his hand tightly, but he loosens his grip.

A muted cheer goes up at his arrival. He disappears,
His family sweeping him into the centre of it all.

She teeters on the edges of the chattering clusters.
Chokes on the toxic-tasting wine, looks for water.

Overhears his cousin ask him, *whatever happened to
That gorgeous bird you used to go out with?*

She says hello to his aunt, who looks at her vaguely,
Then mutters, *my God,* when she reminds her who she is.

Known

To be seen, to be known,
Beyond the gradients, the fractions,
The segments of body that
Now define who she is,
To the people who work this shift.

The sounds and smells of
The radiotherapy unit follow her
For thirty days and nights.
Slip into brain fog as her
Skin reddens, then blisters.

Long after her skin has healed,
She recalls the Radiation
Oncologist's kindness.

Fear

The voltaren has kicked in. Back pain has eased. Still,
Remember the Oncologist said the pain to watch out for
Was the one that woke me in the night?
Osteosarcoma? First signs are bone tenderness.
Can't feel a tumour, though, like Dr Google said I might.

Migraine has passed, thank god. Nauseous, though.
Maybe I don't have a glioblastoma. Still,
I've ticked the first four signs of it!
No incontinence, though, and this unbalanced sensation,
Could be that vestibular disequilibrium, like they said.

This damn black freckle, oh, washed off; dirt!
Melanoma wouldn't surprise me. All that baby oil,
Just to look cool in my teenage tanned skin. Still,
These freckles do look darker, and this one is rough.
My father had skin cancer, but not the hereditary one.

Blood test came back normal; just fatigued.
Wasn't fatigue the first sign that Eve's husband noted?
Myeloid leukemia? Or was it lymphoma? He bled, though.
That cut on my hand has healed, no bruising. Still,
It did really bleed. No, perhaps not that much.

Survivorship

I

I've taken the photos down.
The woman standing on the beach,
Laughing into the camera?

Bad news week – 2008,
Faded ink on the photo paper.
She must have been me.

II

This elusive guilt. I should grasp it,
Wring the haunting life out of it.
It's the voice in my head whispering,

You should be grateful you're here.
The others didn't make it, and
This is the best you can do?

And I stretch and reach,
Chasing the ghost of who I was.
Trying to just hold on.

III

Years later,
At a survivorship conference,
A presenter shone a red laser dot
At the words 'post-traumatic stress disorder'.
And this old survivor,
Long healed from the physical wounds,
Bowed her head and cried.
Yes, bowed her head and cried.

The world in a word

'Benign' is the most
Beautiful of words.

In the surgeon's shorthand scrawl,
Benign: no further action required.

Belies the action I take,
Running in the shallows at Fishos,
Under a swollen, orange moon.

Years ago, I stumbled blindly here,
My world completely engulfed
By malignancy.

Our different ways

He doesn't want to hear the latest news.
He relaxes. Goes about the business
Of daily chores. All the mundane things
We used to complain about.

The surgeon said he got it all, he says,
When I ponder margins and percentages.
He takes what he sees and what he hears
And relishes this getting back to normal.

He didn't go to the chemo ward,
The radiotherapy, the appointments.
Sometimes I wish I hadn't either.
Sometimes I wish I could crawl into a cocoon

Like the one he has spun.
Nestle into the warmth of my bed.
Go to sleep, without the terror,
Wake and complain of the weather.

The morning of the annual mammogram

The night's heavy rain has lifted
The rosemary, the lavender.
Your white cotton shirt,
Limp and damp on the clothesline,
A lymphodematous memory
Trapped in the sodden sleeves.

And the cat, having trekked
The overgrown grass behind the shed,
Delicately licking the
Water from her fur,
Alert for signs of life in the rat
She has dropped at your feet.

After the annual appointment

It must be a skinny latte,
Even though I drink tea now.

And there must be a scone or cake,
Despite the pain it will cause.

Don't ask me to say what would happen
If this plan can't be executed!

I did it the first time, and the second time
It seemed that if I didn't repeat the ritual,

I would be calling the gods down
To wreak their havoc and destroy

Any or all of the equilibrium I had reached,
Where somehow the mutating cells

Had been kept at bay, convinced to not continue
Their deadly inexorable march.

And you see, this less than scientific approach
Has worked because I sit here today

In this little café that didn't even exist
When this craziness began, and I partake of the

Last of these rituals because today was
My final annual appointment at the cancer clinic.

How to describe the essential treatment regime
Of coffee & cake to those who rely solely on science?

Photo

There are two little boys and a young woman
In the photo on the mantelpiece.
And sunshine.

It anchors her day.
This trailing her fingers over the image.
She hears the boys laughing,
Even when they are miles away.

How marvellous her heart is, she thinks.
Beating steadily like the blacksmith's hammer,
Forging something made of love and things unforgotten.
Shaped to suit the times she's titled B.C. (before cancer).

Bramare

I find myself apologising
For being alive,
When all that remains of you
Is this grey stony cairn
At the top of a bush-clad hill.
And love, of course – always love.

The barrel full of brightly
Coloured lottery balls,
Tumbles around and around,
And it is you who is gone,
And me who sits here
In the shadow of a cairn.

Who knows the rationale of
The Grim Reaper's roll call?

Perhaps there isn't one.
Perhaps it's just all in the timing.

A brief note to the oncology nurse

Diagnosed with advanced cancer, August 2019

The barista at the café asked me if that
Cancer you got was that messy kind.
We got to 'metastases' by the time the latte
Was in my hand, and I lied. *I don't know.*

Counting the change into my hand, he mused,
It would make you double think working
As a cancer nurse, if it meant you were going to
Catch the cancer you were chasing in others.

I thought of screaming to no one in particular,
It's all wrong. You, who saved me, now facing
Metastases. With all the changes that matter in life.
Metastasising into the surreally familiar patient

With a poor prognosis. And referrals to all the
Right people and places, to keep you breathing.
To keep your light shining, until it dims into memory.
The discovery of who you are. The farewells.

Mindfulness

1

Everything in this day has been sent to wound me.
A line I could make into poetry, too melodramatic?

I stop to text myself, commit the words to cyberspace.
Better to detach from the drama, reframe into melodic lines.

I creak and click my way around the river track, mentally
Hovering over my body like some vengeful angel seeking pain.

As I pass a magpie and her adolescent chick, a cacophonous duet,
She regurgitates in the way mothers do for their offspring.

This mindfulness they prescribe to me, is a challenge.
Every piece of the present moment engenders bile.

Strikes me with swift shortcuts to poetry. The gaping wound between
Riverbank and the flowing water, lines that twist in unison.

Across the river the thump-thump-thump of adidas trainers on asphalt
Takes me to a slow carriage ride behind a larger-than-life Clydesdale.

A country lane I've never been down, but
The synapses flash in the neuro pathway.

II

A lizard scoots across the path, the rabbit takes his time on his way
To the water. I remember to watch for snakes. I remember poisons.

The counsellor who preaches mindfulness adds that empathy
Does not necessarily require shared experiences.

I ponder if her empathy knows the back pain, the disequilibrium,
The swollen lymphademratous arm, the chronic pain in the hip.

The runners sprint past, scattering the magpie and her young.
They wear V-shaped sweat on their T-shirts like battle shields,

Run in battalion-like batches. I stretch my lips to imply a greeting,
Catch the chorus of mornings, whipped out across the water.

Looking back, I look for rhymes in their swinging, bouncing bodies,
Search for lines about moving, but they speed away out of sight.

Unlike Philip Glass, minimalist masterpiece. Takes me in a vintage car,
Down a long country driveway, streaming sun-stripes through poplar trees.

III

Summer thunder brings me back to the river, I think of lightning strikes.
Determine to be mindful, to comply, or at least try to be honest.

My body scatters into pieces once I stay in the moment, hurts.
I take comfort in the rhythmic splash-splash-splash of kayakers streaming by,

Disappearing behind the scented pine trees.
Rustling; snakes? Are they writing the poisonous lines as I pass?

Cyclists, jangle-jangle, whoosh by. *Thank you*, I call for the warning.
Breathe. The counsellor told me to breathe in, breathe out. Seriously.

Walkers approach in a loud, chatty bunch, fill the track like cockatoos screeching.
Clear a path people, I rage in cerebral angst. Body crunching, like tyres on gravel.

When she told me to breathe, I told the counsellor about the lines,
Lush-edged, verdant verges, on country roads I was travelling down.

With my heart I listen to the waves; my *karanga*

I hate that dog

It comes silently, that black dog of yours.
Arrives in the night on its padded paws.
With a slight whimper, settles into your sleepless body,
Sluices its wet, ugly tongue across your cheek,
Saliva, mucus, and streams of salty waste.

I wake to the silent ute in the driveway.
Cement mixer and tools white with frost, frozen
Immobility, and a silence in the house that
Screams of a mangy presence, that old mongrel musk,
Scenting the descent into your other-world.

Damn that dog. Damn the sun that is pouring in
At the window, defrosting the tools lying
Useless on your truck. As if that will make a difference.

Sometimes

Sometimes, I hear the waves on the beach
Where you walk. You message me
The cold southerly wind. And I breathe
The memory of a sea-weedy stench.

Years ago, in the rockpools, we were brave.
Tidal nights, huddled in the holiday house,
Enfolded in watery lullabies, we slept.
Year after year, summers recycling as
We budded and grew, brown-skinned.

One year I made love in the sand dunes,
Creamy toi-toi and sun, burned into memory.
My first love. My first sea beyond the womb.
Those rocky outcrops running out to the point,
They anchored me, even amidst the betrayals.

At Kaka Point

The *kererū* alights in the *kōwhai* tree.
Too slender a branch surely,
For this crash-landing bird,
But she knows her trees.

Beyond, the slate-grey-white sea,
Disappearing into a darkening night.
And the lighthouse beacon, flashing
Its rhythmic heartbeat.

At St Helen's Park

The secret in the magpie's eye,
Her black stillness. Beak bearing towards
A horizon, grey-steel water and soft sky.

I would seek what she hides, preferring it to the
Punchlines these rainbow lorikeets are laughing
At inanely, in the eucalypts swaying above me.

And the two ant-men, old and fishing on the jetty
Far below, are pointing across the bay, making their
Intelligent observations fly up into the wind stream.

Words buffeted to and fro, some reach me, delayed,
While the Pacific gull, on his slow-motion glide,
Picks at the remains; finds nothing to sustain him.

Something not quite right at St Helen's

I

The wind shrieks through the trees,
Or are the trees shrieking at the wind?
This trust that nature is patterned
As I see it, hear it. Poeticise it.

It's the black swans, surfing the waves
In the Bay, that raise the question.
Where is the graceful ballet upon
Smooth, blue-silvered water?

And now I think the rainbow lorikeets
May have been laughing at me.

II

The red sandstone house on Balmoral Street
Sits like some kind of Spanish hacienda,
In a sun-drenched land, when in reality, it is
Braced against the wind that sweeps up
The Bay, funnelling up the cliff at St. Helens.

On this rare day, its security is abandoned,
The gate, the doors fallen open, inviting
The street walker to peer into the house,
Into the cavernous lungs of the dark interior,
Gaze through it, and out over the grey water beyond.

Dark spots of furniture in the depths of the
House, heavy and malignant in the humid air.

III

The old church on Balmoral Street
Has been removed, or demolished.
The hall has been left. Its wounded side
Broken and open, black spaces where
Stained-glass eyes had captured light.

The panes of coloured stories; growths
That were surgically removed, destroyed.
There will be reconstruction of course,
Something new and iron-dull; modern
Slatted windows that will repel the light.

A black fence has been erected around
The perimeter of the building site.
Two local cats are inspecting the ruins,
Blatantly ignoring the warning signs;
No entry for unauthorised persons.

Or perhaps not? On closer inspection,
The tabby cat, impressive white bib,
Looks to have the authority to be there,
Or anywhere he chooses to go on his
Official business as neighbourhood cat.

Local historians, they step daintily,
Cautiously, through the rubble,
Methodically recording the denuding
In some efficient feline filing system,
Wisely entitled *Cancerous human activity.*

III Postscript

And now the half-hall has gone,
Or rather, it was taken when I
Turned my head and walked away.
No cats, or rubble, just ground laid bare.

I stand and glare at the digger driver,
Excavating a hole for the underground
Foundations on a cliff where once,
People came to an old church to pray.

Stringing words together

The oncologist with the bright eyes, talked of a miracle.
She kept saying, *it's a miracle*, and now the word sits there,

Lit up like some static neon sign, not pulsating but bright enough
That I wish I'd worn my sunglasses, or that she'd never uttered it.

I know the fragility of miracles, my friend wrote. Is it core business
For him, the spiritual leader? Or is a sacred monopoly so yesterday?

Intentional. There are other words that go with my friend's job title,
But that's the one I choose to remember. And his kindness.

I'm becoming a one-word bandit. Allows me to cut through the crap,
Through all the red tape of rambling sentences.

If I look up at what is carved up there in the sky by the
Outline of trees against skimming clouds, against a strange light,

I can see where all this is leading to. I get it now.
Once a word is spoken, it haunts, like a ghost of itself.

*

Hey, I know. We could play this game
Where we speak to each other using single words.
Don't make it a word association thing!
Like, if I say

Transformation, don't be tempted to
Leap in and yell, WTF!
Because strictly speaking, that's not a word,
Despite its associated truth.

The angel cards come out in threes,
Because that's my number.
Although the willowware angels on the bookcase
Sit in a group of four.

I did that deliberately to challenge
My need for stability. It didn't work.
But which angel should I risk
Losing for the sake of restoring order?

My cards yesterday. Truth. Play. Adventure.
Adventure angel is climbing a mountain,
It's a cosmic joke, right?
She has wings but she chooses to do the hard climb!

Did you see how I sidestepped the first two cards?
Don't be expecting me
To even begin to speak the truth.
I tried that, once. I lost everything.

*

Look, I've decided to gather all these
One-word stories and string them together
On a silver thread. Because I think
I'll wear them round my neck,

Like an heirloom that's been
Handed down to me, by all those women
Who went before me; the ones who taught me to
Bury words deep within me.

These damn words. They're heavy,
But I keep stringing them together.
I try them on, risking the strangulation.
They're a heavy burden.

But like the smear of cells under a microscope,
They were there before I knew
The damage they could do. Haunting me.
Randomly, I select my angel cards.

Grace. Love. Surrender. Grace is depicted as a ballerina,
While love is all hearts.
And the surrender angel?
Another mountain, and she's a white flag waving.

*

I carved a word into the wallpaper above my childhood bed.
I did it for permanency. I don't remember the word.

Reading the graffiti flying by, on a train to Melbourne.
Hey, I get it, dude! Dude, what a ridiculous word. But it slips out.

This haunting dictionary my body carries within its cells,
Is a daily reminder of the verbal need to clarify the chaos.

Long after the wallpaper has been stripped away from the wall,
And replaced with pastel paint. Long after the train has sped

Past the concrete warehouses with their sad, spray-painted faces,
The hypnotic, addictive need to explain continues.

The heaviest word; the one in the wallpaper above the bed.
Might as well be a neon sign, although I hide its brightness well.

I said I didn't remember it; the word. I wasn't lying, more trying to
enact the miracle; to pretend that I could separate myself from it.

Walking the perimeter

The people sitting
On the park benches
Outside the hospital,
Brazenly blowing
Their smoke at me
As I pass by.

The paramedics wrestling
A desperate man,
In the ambulance bay.
Stripped to his underpants,
Screaming he's on fire,
Burning up, on ice.

The man with a red mohawk
Sifting through the
Rubbish bin for butts,
Striking gold,
With an angelic smile.
You bloody beauty!

A woman on a walking frame
At the entrance to
The Cancer Centre,
Half her face missing,
Swathed in bandages,
Grumbling at the taxi driver.

Driving the perimeter

I

On the road to Portland, a fox stands poised,
Looking back across the paddocks at
Something a fox would look at. I brake.
Gauging the speed of the oncoming car,
I freeze, but the fox runs. Leaves a flash
Of brown life, disappears into long grass.

On a winter's moonlit night at Haven Court,
A fox made its loping run across the grassland
Below our house. I sat at the upstairs window,
Crouched silent with the foreign night.
The fox froze, and our eyes
Met in a long, exquisite moment.

II

The dahlia show is on in Portland,
Gardens dew-wet and glowing colours,
Exquisite shapes perfectly formed,
Removed from the deadly space.

Beyond, the ache that sits
Close and sad in the stillness,
Lost like treasures in a sack, left
In the corridors of the hospital.

Where the woman, twenty-five,
And a mother of two,
Shone brightly, then disappeared.
Gone, while the staff went on

Tapping the chemo bags and diligently
Writing the notes of condolence
In their morning tea break.
Stoic amidst the vases.

III

It is messy living in a small town
When your lover finds the lump,

And the only place to sit by a pump
Of toxic, death-defying chemicals,

Is the chair that is under your
Watchful care, as you tell the

Other patients you're holding
His hand because he's your man.

And they marvel at the way you can be
The lover, the nurse, all rolled into one.

All the trees

Pungent, sap-weeping stumps line up
In an orange row, at the back of the farm,
While fencers, flashing black eyes,
Musky-shiny bodies, drink sugary tea.

Pine trees fall near Gilbert Street, where
Woolworths will squat in an asphalt bed.
Stillness in Taylor Park, beyond the sea,
Petulant rip-whining of chainsaws.

Roots wither and die under the tree stump
Painted yellow, in the nature strip at no. 10.
Beside it, the sister-tree bends its limbs,
Brushes the brass plaque, 'Two Trees'.

Why do we hold ourselves apart from trees,
The interconnections between this one,
And the next one? If only we could
Rise above ourselves, the way trees do.

Evening walk during lockdown

A cornucopia of words spiralling
Up out of the horn of my body,
Abundant and lush, each one
Vying for a place within the poem.

Must surely be the posture of
The trailing willow limbs, graceful
In the passing garden, or the day's
Residue of meditative light.

But now enter a man and a woman,
At the corner of the evening park.
I have been trying to understand!
Her anger, excoriating.

They stand socially, acceptably apart,
In intimate, isolated proximity.
Only, their words are stabbing deeply,
Leaving wounds for the night to swallow.

And I am left with the emptiness
Of lapping water on slimy rocks
Down on the bay, and a foghorn
Sounding from a distant ship.

Caught between

Those waves lapping down at the shore,
Once ran themselves up against the black bones
Of Moeraki; were thrust back across the ocean.

And this moon, sullen in the crack between
My open window and the broken-down fence,
Turned pale, insignificant before Aoraki.

Before now I believed I could join them.
With my supernatural energy and a compass,
I could leap into the abyss, destroy all in the past.

Do battle with the bunyip who dared to invade
The long twisting bone of the taniwha. Cancer,
Itself a fearsome foe, caught me in the divide.

Silenced the wind in the tallest of the totara,
While the eucalypt continued to murmur its crackling heat.
With my heart, I listen to the waves; my *karanga*.

Acknowledgements

Some of these poems have been previously published as follows:

'Forgiveness', *Lothlorien Poetry Journal*, https://lothlorienpoetry journal.blogspot.com/2021/10/five-poems-by-heather-cameron.html, 12 October 2021

'The problem with soup', *Lothlorien Poetry Journal*, https://lothlorien poetryjournal.blogspot.com/2021/10/five-poems-by-heather-cameron.html, 12 October 2021

'This play of ours', *Lothlorien Poetry Journal*, https://lothlorien poetryjournal.blogspot.com/2021/10/five-poems-by-heather-cameron.html, 12 October 2021

'My hair', *Lothlorien Poetry Journal*, https://lothlorienpoetry journal.blogspot.com/2021/10/five-poems-by-heather-cameron.html, 12 October 2021

'In the chemo chair', *Lothlorien Poetry Journal*, https://lothlorien poetryjournal.blogspot.com/2021/10/five-poems-by-heather-cameron.html, 12 October 2021

'Cancer', *The Write Launch*, https://thewritelaunch.com, 4 October 2021

'Where it starts', *The Write Launch*, https://thewritelaunch.com, 4 October 2021

'Anatomy of disaster', *The Write Launch*, https://thewritelaunch.com, 4 October 2021

'Everything', *Snapdragon – A Journal of Art and Healing*, Fall 2021

'A death on the way to day chemo', Spillwords.com, https://spillwords.com/a-death-on-the-way-to-day-chemo/, 4 September 2021

'A random caller', *A Fleeting Visitor*, Poets Choice, https://www.poetschoice.in/, June 2021

'Waiting room', *A Fleeting Visitor*, Poets Choice, https://www.poetschoice.in/, June 2021

'After you died', Spillwords.com, https://spillwords.com/after-you-died, 11 June 2021

'Note to the young doctor', *Please See Me*, issue 6, Fall 2020

'The memory of kindness', *Best of Kindness 2020*, J. Keough & K. Keough (eds), independently published, October 2020

'Fear', *Medical Journal of Australia* (MJA), vol. 213, no. 11, December 2020

'Breast cancer 2', *British Journal of Medical Practitioners* (BJMP), vol. 13, no. 1, July 2020

'#2' (earlier version of 'Survivorship II'), *Alluvia*, http://alluvia.nz/read/poetry/, issue 1, 2017

'So what was chemo like?' (earlier version), *Atlas*, issue 01, 2016

www.ingramcontent.com/pod-product-compliance
Lightning Source LLC
Chambersburg PA
CBHW050255120526
44590CB00016B/2357